Never Mind, Comrade

Never Mind, Comrade

life behind the iron curtain 1982-89

Claudia Bierschenk

with a foreword by **Pete Lally**

TANGERINE PRESS · LONDON · 2022

Originally published in German as LAND OHNE VERBEN
COPYRIGHT © 2020 THE AUTHOR & EDITION ÜBERLAND, mbH

ISBN 978-1-910691-70-0 (paperback)
   978-1-910691-71-7 (hardback)

NEVER MIND, COMRADE. COPYRIGHT © 2022 CLAUDIA BIERSCHENK
FOREWORD. COPYRIGHT © 2022 PETE LALLY
THIS EDITION FIRST PUBLISHED 2022 BY TANGERINE PRESS
UNIT 18
RIVERSIDE ROAD
GARRATT BUSINESS PARK
LONDON
SW17 0BA
ENGLAND
thetangerinepress.com
PRINTED IN ENGLAND
ALL RIGHTS RESERVED

Tangerine Press books are printed on acid-free paper

Publisher's Note & Acknowledgements

Grateful acknowledgement is given to the editors of the publications where the following sections first appeared: 'The American' (alternate version, with the title 'The First American') and 'Bright yellow underpants' (with the title 'The Beautifullest') in *Pure Slush*; 'Baba' (with the title 'Baba Yaga') in *Witch-pricker*; 'The fence is just a fence' (with the title 'November 10, 1989') in *Fool-saint*. The author and publisher also wish to extend their gratitude to Hans Ticha, who kindly permitted the use of his artwork in the limited editions of this book.

Never Mind, Comrade is not a direct translation of *Land ohne Verben*. Both the German and English language versions have been developed in parallel by the author, with sections added and removed in the English version, as the author saw fit, for a wider international readership.

Foreword

I first met Claudia Bierschenk on a cold and grey winter's day at a train station on the eastern side of Berlin in 2013. At this point in our shared history I had published some of her poems in a journal of new writing and illustration, with this relationship developing in later years to include a short poetry collection.

I was in the city for a book launch and we decided it would be a good opportunity to meet in person. Having made our way back to her apartment, I was fascinated by her *Kachelofen* which seemed so alien and yet so charming to me, the tiled stove providing warmth as we shared tea and biscuits and talked about the forthcoming birth of her son, Luther. We also talked about her life as a child growing up behind the 'iron curtain' and how, despite the unquestionable challenges this presented, it still brought people together, something that was perhaps missing in the present times where many lead increasingly isolated lives.

This uneasy and often contradictory relationship with the state and its rules and regulations comes through in *Never Mind, Comrade*. The collection of distant memories that follow often belies the grey surroundings of the former East Germany and paints vivid pictures of a young girl defiantly pushing her small cart through the streets of a changing world where nothing is certain, everything is questioned and family is all.

A few years after our meeting Claudia told me that Luther would often ask for stories from the "War Country" and how she would sing him to sleep with East German dissident songs, so perhaps it is this young man who we should be most thankful to for this book.

— Pete Lally

*For Luther: when you see a
fence, climb over it*

Never Mind, Comrade

EAST

The Sting

Most of my clothes are hand-me-downs from our relatives in West Germany. They send us care parcels with things we cannot buy here. Things they do not need any more, but which are of great value to us. But for my first day at school, my mother made me a skirt from a shiny fabric with flower prints. I call it my "meadow skirt", because when I twirl in it, it looks like a meadow in early summer. The first day at school is only an hour long. We sit on small hard chairs in the auditorium, with our hands in our laps and listen to the headmaster's speech. I don't know what he's talking about. We look and listen as the older students sing about unity, socialism, and friendship between all peace-loving nations of the world. The older students are wearing white shirts and red neckerchiefs, the "Pioniertuch", or dark blue shirts with the symbol of the Free German Youth on the sleeve: a rising sun above the letters FDJ. They all look so grown up. I cannot imagine that one day I will be as old as they are and wear such a blue shirt, maybe have my hair permed, and blue eyeshadow. I cannot imagine that I will be any different from what I am right now. When all the speeches and singing are done, we are called to the front, one by one, and are handed our "sugar cones": large, colourful cardboard cones, taller than us, filled to the brim with goodies. I am sure that in my sugar cone, there'll be plenty of little presents from my aunt from West Berlin. I would love to run home right now and spill it on the living room floor, but first, we have to assemble in the courtyard outside for the photo session. When it's my turn, the photographer takes ages to get me into the right position. The

hands should go here, one foot there, a slight turn of the head. It's hot and the sun is glaring, but he tells me not to squint. I need to remember to not smile, so that my crooked teeth won't show. I am good at not smiling. Suddenly, just as the photographer is happy with how and where I am standing, I can feel something crawling on my right hand. It's thick and warm and has many legs. And then a pain flashes through my finger into my hand, my arm and through my body. I can feel my eyes filling up, but I must not cry now. I blink away the tears and force my mouth into a tight-lipped smile.

Edge of the world

I live at the edge of a world called the German Democratic Republic, in a village surrounded by hills, valleys and thick forests. It could be beautiful, but the iron curtain runs through it like a scar, and we just so happen to live on the wrong side of it. Or on the right side, depending how you look at it. The whole world talks about the Berlin Wall, and about Berlin, the divided city. And I don't know what the fuss is about, when here, along this border; entire villages are cut in half, as are the families who live there. In East Berlin, the shop shelves are fully stocked, I saw it myself when we went there for a visit. They have more than two flavours of yogurt. In East Berlin, they have bananas and cornflakes, and nothing is rationed.

If you travel through our village eastwards, the main road leads to the great wide world German Democratic Republic. Hardly anyone travels the road west. It's the mystery road, because once

you reach the village limit sign it's less than one kilometre to the first border checkpoint. From there, it's not far to the Fence, which is what we call the border. At school, I am told the Fence is there to protect us, but my parents and some other adults I know say it's to keep us in. I have learnt to ignore it, like I ignore empty shelves in the shops, drunk men on a Saturday morning in the village park, the rundown houses, the overpowering greyness of everything, dotted with party slogan posters, the windows darkened by a constant outpour of soot from coal furnaces, the polluted river, illegal rubbish dumps. Because of the Fence, I can believe in two contradictory things at the same time. I can believe in God *and* the Socialist Unity Party. But of course, I only pretend I do, because really, I only believe what I see on the illegal West German TV channels. I am constantly told I am too young for this and that, but I already know exactly what to say where, when and to whom. I know that we are all hacks and we despise hacks. We complain behind closed doors. We always feel a bit guilty and a bit scared. We are cowards.

Privileges

The first year at school is hell. I am scared of our head teacher, who explodes with rage when someone talks in class and she likes to whack the talker around the head with a stack of books. Occasionally she'll throw her keys, aiming right at the head. Because that is where our stupidity sits. On a good day, she'll just throw bits of chalk. Her voice rattles from decades of smoking and shouting. Then again, she is sometimes extra

nice to me, because my father is a teacher, too, and they are colleagues. But I am still scared of her rage. I sit with my knees together and my arms folded, so stiff and still my muscles start to ache. I dare not look up at the window or turn around or talk to my neighbour, because I don't want to anger her and be told off. I am scared of anger.

During first recess, two pupils go to fetch the crate with milk bottles. The bottles are quite large and for some of us, it's a lot of milk to finish in a ten-minute break. But we need to drink it all, because we have the privilege of getting this milk for free. Children in capitalist countries aren't so lucky. If someone dares to put the bottle back into the crate and there is a drop left, the teacher has us line up. We each have to pick out our bottle from the crate and then the perpetrator who hasn't finished their milk has to drink the rest of it and they get a black dot by their name in the class book. I always remember exactly where I put my bottle in the crate. After morning lessons, we all go for our school lunch and again, we have to finish our plates, everything, whether you like it or not, whether you're full or not, whether it's steamed kidneys or liver, or tripe, we have to eat it all. We are so lucky because we get this good, warm meal every day for a laughable fee of one Mark a month or something like that, and we had better eat it all. We cannot leave the table until our plates are empty.

Red dots, black dots

After lunch, we are ordered to nap. Because napping is good, it gives us strength, and whether we are tired or not, we have to lie down on the wooden plank beds in the school's dorm. I see traces of sunshine peeking through the gaps in the dark curtains, and all I want is to be outside riding my bike through the village, but I have to be in here in the dark in the middle of the day for at least an hour and pretend I'm asleep. I don't know how the others do it. They lie down and close their eyes, but I can't, so I sit up on my bed. The head teacher, who's watching us, instantly hisses at me, *Lie down or else!* I shake my head in a sudden fit of rebellion. I don't want to lie down. *You'll never get your six red dots!* she hisses back at me and I shrug. We get black dots for bad behaviour and red dots for good behaviour. The pupils who fall asleep nicely, lying on their back with their arms on top of the blanket, get red dots, and when they have six red dots, they can go outside and play during naptime. So, I ask myself, if the reward for good behaviour is not having to take a nap, is napping a punishment for something? One afternoon, after naptime, when I can finally, finally go home, the teacher reads out who still needs how many points: *Maik still needs one point, Conny needs one point, Silvio two points, Claudia five points.* Shame hits me like a wet, cold cloth.

It's voluntary

It's time for us to join the Young Pioneers, one of East Germany's three main youth organisations. I have no idea what changes when we become Young Pioneers, other than we now have to wear a blue neckerchief tied in a very specific knot, the so-called "Pioneer knot". It symbolises the strong bond between us and our Big Brother, the Soviet Union. We have a specific greeting: we hold our hand over our head, like a shark's fin, our fingers symbolising the friendship between children from all five continents, because children are innocent, all over the world. They only become our class enemy once they grow up. I don't know how that is possible, but it seems to be true. Joining the Pioneers is supposedly voluntary, says my mother. I can join, but I don't have to. However, it would make things easier, so much easier if I just joined, like everyone else. Our family really doesn't need any more attention. I don't feel too good about this. I have a feeling that the ceremony for joining the Young Pioneers will upset my daily schedule and that I won't be able to come straight home after school.

Are you sure I can come home as always today, Mama?
Yes, of course, why shouldn't you?

But at the end of the last lesson before lunchtime, one of the educators comes into the classroom carrying a stack of blue neckerchiefs, whispers something to our teacher and they disappear into the adjacent office. A few minutes later, the office door opens again and the head teacher calls me in. Shame and fear run their electric currents from my stomach to my throat as I slowly rise from my chair. I can feel the heat pounding in my

head as I stand before these two women who look at me blankly, and one of them, I don't know who, says, *You cannot go home after lunch today*.

The heat in my head now pushes tears into my eyes and I can see how they're both rolling their eyes behind these impossibly large glasses and one of them lets out that familiar sigh of annoyance so typical of most adults I have to deal with. I know there is no room for negotiation here. I must stay in this place that I hate so much and join the Pioneers like the others, who don't even question it. As I walk back to my seat, someone calls out: *She's crying again*. I sit down and say nothing. What is wrong with me? Why are the others all so accepting of everything that's going on here? And why do they feel so uncomfortable when I am unhappy? Not once, not once does a teacher or educator at my school ask me what is going on with me, and if there is anything I need. Not once. I am not functioning as I should and that is a threat. I join the Pioneers in this semi-sacred ritual in the festively decorated common room in the basement, where we have to repeat the oath and swear allegiance on the red flag. And then I can finally leave. As I turn the corner towards home, the wind plays with my blue neckerchief and a passer-by says, *Look at that, a Young Pioneer!*

The restricted zone

We have a permit to travel into the Zone for an uncle's birthday. The Zone is still in East Germany, but it's so close to the border fence that everyone needs a permit to get in and get out.

In our black and yellow Lada, we travel along the potholed mystery street, up the hill and down again until we stop at the first checkpoint. It looks like a rundown bus stop, with a red and white barrier. Two grey-green uniformed soldiers wave at us. *Hello, how are you?* They know my parents, of course. My father is a teacher and these two very young guards were probably in his class. My stomach tickles as we pass the checkpoint barrier and drive along the narrow, windy road. My father drives slowly, carefully, as if he's afraid he'll do something wrong and they will yell at him to stop. *There it is*, he says, points to the Fence that winds its way up the hill and disappears into the forest. We are so close to the West, we could just cross the field, really hit the gas pedal and drive right through it, right through and over to the other side! But we cannot, because my little sister is not in the car with us. She has to stay at home with my grandmother, because they only issued a permit for my mother, my father and myself. My grandfather, who is also with us, doesn't need one, because at the age of seventy-nine he wouldn't be missed if he defected. Grandfather is sitting in the front passenger seat and hasn't said a word. But now he speaks. *Before they built the fence, I used to walk all the way from my home village to work. And then they built the fence, and I couldn't do that anymore.*

The last house before the fence

The villages in the Zone are dirty and brittle. I didn't think it was possible that there were places even more run down than where we live. The relatives we're going to visit live in the last

house before the Fence. There it is, behind the garden hedge and the plum trees. How high? Six metres? Ten metres? It has barbed wire on top, and green and red alarm lights. The uncle, who has come to meet us at the gate, drags on his cigarette and tells us about "Rabbit discos", which happens every time an animal touches the trip wire and then, *They come running like cattle, with their Kalashnikovs*. He chuckles. We stand there and stare at the Fence.

    I know my mother is looking at the world beyond this metal monstrosity. At the fields and the forest, at the horizon. I know she constantly dreams about that world, and how much she wants to be there, and the only thing holding her back is my sister and I. I know that my father already thinks about whether we'll be back home on time so he can go to Judo training. I look at the grass growing on this side and on the other side, and the grass that is growing through the Fence. It must have roots in the East, and then it grows over to the West. Where does it belong? I know I will never ever touch the grass on the other side. This is our reality: we are standing here, on this side. For the first time, I feel really, really helpless. I know where our place is. And there is nothing that my parents or I can do about it. The barbed wire, the trip wires, the signals, they are for us. The feeling gets too big for my body, it makes a knot in my chest, and I am relieved when my mother says she wants to go inside, because she's wearing a red jumper and is convinced that the border troops have already spotted and photographed her.

Here and there

I don't know anyone in the village who doesn't watch the West German television channels. It's illegal, of course, but everyone does it. I need to switch over to the East German channel or better, turn the television off, when the doorbell rings on a Saturday evening around six o'clock. This is the time when the local people's police officer or even the mayor calls to check on us. A friendly visit, just to see how things are. Maybe ask about who that BMW belonged to that parked outside our house the week before. People act as if they were indifferent about the West. But there's hardly anyone here who does not have family "over there". There's always some West German car parked outside someone's house, and the curtains are drawn aside when the low humming of a diesel engine echoes through the street. At every christening, wedding, funeral, people anxiously await the arrival of their West German relatives. It's always about "over there" and "over here", staying, going, for the cause, against the cause. It could drive you crazy.

Fidel's revenge

I have the flu and am ordered to stay in bed. My mother brings me a little bowl full of the sweet, tinned freshness of tangerine slices. Small orange sailing boats capsized in sugary water.

Tinned fruit is sacred and only opened when one of us is sick. I savour each slice, move it around in my mouth, and suck all the juice out of it. Then I sip the juice from the bowl, slowly, so

it lasts. My mother washes and dries the tin, then holds it over a pot of boiling water so the steam slowly peels off the colourful label with a picture of real tangerines on a tangerine tree, and I keep the label as a bookmark. I have labels with pineapples, peaches and tangerines. In our country, you cannot buy exotic, tinned fruit just like that. Bananas are available once a year in the local shop, mostly at Christmas, and they are of course rationed, like tomatoes and oranges. The only oranges that are not rationed are the ones imported from Cuba, one of our brother countries. These oranges aren't orange, but a deep green and we call them "Fidel's revenge", because they often give us stomach cramps and diarrhoea. We ignore that and eat them anyway.

Pull a blanket over it

Most of our family managed to make it over to West Germany or West Berlin before or after the Fence and the Wall were built. My parents, my sister and I are still here, as are my grandparents, and some other grey-faced relatives I hardly know. We are lucky, because our Western relatives send over plenty of care parcels, filled with new bed sheets, tights, coffee, fruit and fruit juice. Not everyone gets that many parcels. We can always tell when the border guards have opened them, because it looks like a five year old re-packed them. Printed magazines are of course illegal, and my aunt wraps them in aluminium foil, thinking the scanner at the border control won't spot them. It is my personal privilege to pick up the parcels from the post office, in the little pushcart. I am so proud when I wheel them through the whole village,

past the bakery, the shop, the petrol station. Everyone can see. I want everyone to see. *Pull a blanket over it!* says my grandmother.

Coconut

One day, my aunt from West Berlin sends us a care parcel that has a real coconut in it! I want to take it to class and show it off to my friends, but my parents won't allow it, in case it's illegal. We save the coconut for a few weeks and put it on the kitchen shelf for everyone to see. Then one day, I see a commercial on the West German channel that blows me away: a beautiful woman with long blond hair and a flowing white dress walks along a beach. My God, are there really beaches like that in the world? The sand is almost white, the sea is turquoise and palm trees are swaying in the breeze. The beautiful woman is a little careless, because the wind blows off her white, elegant hat. A handsome man with white teeth catches it for her and then he offers her a coconut that he has managed to open somehow while she wasn't looking. She holds up the coconut and a stream of milk flows from it right into a glass that has appeared out of nowhere. I decide it's time to slaughter the nut. My parents and I sit around it and we have no idea what to do. I suggest fetching the hatchet that grandfather uses to kill the chickens, but my father gets a screwdriver and drills a couple of holes into what look like dents in the nut. Nothing comes out. The nut is dry. He takes it outside and smashes it on the stone slabs in the courtyard. It shatters into five large pieces. There is nothing in it; it is hollow, lined with dry white skin that has shrivelled like toes after a long bath.

Such a fine man

On Saturday evenings, I usually sit upstairs in my grandparents' small living room and we watch a family show on one of the West German channels. Grandfather snoozes in his armchair, and Grandmother crochets.

She makes triangular or rectangular coasters for neighbours, acquaintances, and West German relatives. She gave up teaching me how to do it a long time ago, because I lack talent and patience. I make long crochet-threads, because I'm not so interested in the result, I just like the movement of the needle. While grandmother's working on her coasters, she misses nothing on the screen, where the famous West German host Hans-Joachim Kuhlenkampff is announcing the next show act. *What a lovely man, this Herr Kuhlenkampff, such a nice suit, and his shoes are always so nicely polished!* My grandfather scoffs. *Did you know he was in Stalingrad?*

Grandmother gives me advice

If you swallow a dog's hair, you'll get a colon blockage and you will die, if you drink water after eating cherries, you can die, if you drink water after eating warm cake, your belly will swell up, if you go swimming after eating, you can drown, if you sit under a lamp during a thunderstorm, lightning will strike you, don't touch a cat's nose, you'll get worms and might die, dry your hair really well after washing it, or you'll get terribly sick and you might die, you'll live to see the third world war, but we won't.

Fears

I have many scary thoughts:

I am going to die from one of the illnesses grandmother talks about all the time,

My mother will not come back from her visit to West Germany,

My parents will get a divorce,

The third world war is coming,

I will say the wrong thing to the wrong person,

My father is arrested for saying something wrong to the wrong person.

Tell me about the war

Opa, tell me about the war.

What can I tell you, it was bad, really bad. The partisans were the worst.

But the partisans were your friends, right? You fought together against Hitler, didn't you?

I want to look at the album again, the one with black and white photos of my father when he was little, and of my grandparents' wedding day. But most of all, I want to see the photo of my grandfather in the desert in Africa. He is holding a camel by the reins. He looks right at the camera and he's not smiling. I want him to tell me about the desert, the sand, and how a scorpion stung him. It was a white scorpion that had hid

in his sleeve. I cannot believe that all he got was an injection and he was fine again. To me, the scorpion sting seems more dangerous than guns. I want to know if it hurts, how it hurts and he has to tell me again and again how it hid in his coat sleeve.

He spent three years in Africa during the war, near Tripoli. He pronounces it "Trippolis". He tells me everything about the journey to Trippolis, but he never mentions the word "Africa Corps". Later in the war, he was sent to the Eastern Front, to Orscha in Belarus. He doesn't like to talk about that. *Sweetie, why do you want to know these terrible things?* For a long time, I am not sure in which army my grandfather fought and for what. At school, we learn that the war is something we have put behind us. It is the responsibility of the West German government now, because we are all Anti-fascists. There are no Nazis in East Germany.

There are no Nazis in East Germany

Someone has scratched a swastika into a desk in our classroom. We stand around it and no one says anything, because we are all petrified. It has to be one of us, because no one else uses this classroom, only we do. This is the unthinkable, the ultimate taboo, worse than defecting to the West, almost as bad as saying out loud "Honecker is an idiot!" Who in their right mind would do that? There are no Nazis in East Germany, only in West Germany.

Then the Russians came

Grandfather had not lost any limbs in Belarus. He brought back with him: a grenade splinter lodged in his elbow, silence, an extraordinary sense for order and tidiness.

There were other grandfathers in the village who had lost an arm, a leg, an eye, in the war. To me "lost" sounds as if they had left it behind by accident. It sounds like "I just happened to be there and lost it". Frozen off fingers and toes are scattered in Ukrainian fertile soil, the "breadbasket of the Soviet Union" as we learn at school. We don't talk about what exactly our grandfathers were doing there. Occasionally, very rarely, it is a topic at home, and only when I ask questions.

Uncle Alois, when he came back from the Camp, he looked like a skeleton. You could blow a prayer through his ribcage.

What camp?

A prisoner of war camp in Siberia.

But why was he a prisoner in the Soviet Union?

We could already see the spires of Moscow, we were that close.

Why did you go to Moscow, to fight Hitler's army who was already there?

(Laughter)

What happened then?

Then the Russians came.

Black Dog

Whenever I ask my grandfather to tell me the story of the black dog, he shudders. He doesn't like to, but he tells me anyway.

This was before I went to war, long before the fence was built.

Every morning, every evening, I walked from my home village to work and back. And always through the forest, you know that curvy road, and it goes up very steep and then down down down. So one evening I was late, and it was getting dark, and I didn't like being in the forest in the dark. I never liked the evening light, the time before the sun goes down. Everything looks unreal in that light.

So, I was walking, and suddenly the little hairs on the back of my neck were standing up. I can feel there is something behind me so I turn around and there is this huge black dog just standing there looking at me! I got a terrible chill down my spine and my heart was beating very fast. And I called to it "Get away from me, you devil", and it jumped in the ditch and was gone. I held my walking stick tight and went to check but he was just gone. I ran home the rest of the way. I tell you, that was the devil, I am sure of it.

Choices

I'm on my way to the butcher's, which is at the far side of the village. I go past the shops, along the deserted main street, across the bridge over the stinking river that is foaming with sewage and industrial waste, past Bruno's kiosk, the school, and the petrol station. And there's my favourite place in the whole world,

the post office. The post office is one small, dark room, and you have to walk up a very steep flight of stairs. This is where I go to collect the care parcels my aunt sends from West Berlin. I put them on a little push cart and walk proudly back through the village. Grandmother always tells me to cover them up so no one sees that we get so many of them. I don't think it's because she's afraid that the authorities might keep an even closer eye on us. I think it's against her Catholic ideas.

But today the post office is closed. I'm on my way to the butcher's, and I can already see the long queue of people as I turn the corner. We queue a lot in this country. We have no telephones, but word goes out fast whenever there's something special to be had in the shop. *There's a shipment of bananas in the shop today!* Queue. *There's a shipment of cornflakes, two bags each!* Queue. If you're lucky, and the shopkeeper likes you or owes you a favour, they might save you your ration in case you don't have the time for queuing.

The walls, floor and ceiling of the butcher shop are covered in white tiles. Pink cold cuts are displayed on scratched aluminium trays. Big chunks of pale meat hang from iron hooks. The butcher woman's face is pink too, she looks stressed and sweaty and takes my list: six slices of cold cuts, three slices of ham, half a pound of beef for soup. *Cheap beef or expensive beef?* She asks me. I don't know. I wasn't prepared for that question. How much is expensive? It's rare that I get a choice, so I don't know what to say. The expensive beef has less fatty white tendons in it. *For soup you can use the cheap beef*, she says. I'm relieved. Again, someone has decided something for me.

Phone aunt

It's already dark outside as my mother and I run next door to Else's in our slippers. The streetlights haven't been turned on yet or maybe they're broken again. At Else's, we stumble up the stairs into the small living room, where her husband's thin body is barely visible on the worn out sofa. He mumbles a greeting and is not happy that we are once again disrupting his peace. Mostly he's not happy that my aunt from West Berlin calls us on his phone, because who knows when this might all backfire on him.

There, on a side table, is the apparatus that is as rare in these parts as coconuts – the telephone. Else and her husband are among a handful of fortunate people (the doctor, the mayor, the priest, the policeman) who have a telephone, because her husband is a paramedic. They are not allowed to *make* phone calls themselves, only *receive* them. For every personal phone call they make, they have to give a precise and valid reason in writing and then hand it in somewhere, I don't know where. My mother is out of breath, hungry for her sister's voice from the big wide free world. I sit patiently on the hard stool next to the phone waiting my turn. Then I hear my aunt's voice in what feels several continents away, in West Berlin. There is much creaking, swishing and murmuring in the line.

Hello my love, how are you?
Fine, thank you.
How is school?
It's okay.

I want to ask her so much. I want to ask her if she can send me a Tina Turner record, or a real pineapple, and what it's

like in Italy. But I am not sure if this is okay, if there might be consequences, so I just answer her questions and then hand back the phone to my mother.

I want to be what you are

The fact that I am not baptised is a big problem for my grandmother. *The child must be baptised. Imagine she dies – then we cannot bury her in our cemetery!*

So one night, before my mother tucks me in, she says, it would be better if I were baptised. Grandmother won't stop going on about it. And to be baptised is actually good, because it would be an official occasion where my aunt and cousins from West Berlin might be able to visit and I would probably get a lot of West German Marks and lots of presents! And I could choose if I wanted to be Protestant or Catholic. I look at her and go through the pros and cons of baptism in my head. Then I say, *I want to be what you are.*

Treasures

Herr Rosenstock runs the best shop in the village, a book and paper shop. I go there at least once a week and exchange my pocket money for books, which are very cheap in this country. All I have to say to my parents is that I saw something interesting in Herr Rosenstock's shop window and I really need to have it, and my parents never say no to me buying a book. My father has

hundreds of them stacked to the ceiling in our living room and I want just as many as he has.

I take out books from the library, but really, I just want to own them. I want to hold them, smell the pages, be the only one to read this book, the first one to open its pages. Herr Rosenstock has subjects on everything that interests me: the oceans, insects, Aztecs, photography, anatomy. He is my king of books, with his wavy grey hair, a grey work coat, pale face, and the kindest eyes. He calls me "little Bookworm". When he hands me my newly chosen treasure over the counter, we smile at each other, because he only ever has one copy, no one else but I will have this book. My favourite ones are by the great East German ethnologist Erich Wustmann, who writes about his travels to the Amazon, to North American Indians, to the desert. One question bugs me. How did Erich Wustmann get to these places? What did he have to do so they let him travel to these far away and forbidden places? From what I know, no one can travel anywhere other than our socialist brother countries, so how could he travel to the Amazon? *Papa, can I become an ethnologist like him and then travel to these places? I don't know,* says my father. *I don't know.*

Grenades

I am more interested in how things work, and not so much in the result of processes. And that is a problem, since we're always pushed for better and better results, mostly in sports competitions. Who gets the best grades, who jumps higher and runs faster. And it is all for "the cause", this strange, undefinable

thing that is all around us and in everything we do. I have no idea what "the cause" is. I think it has to do with the October Revolution in Russia in 1917, because apparently, this revolution is still ongoing, but I don't understand how that is possible. One day, our physical education teacher hands us defused hand grenades so we can practice throwing them. We have to try and throw them as far as possible, which isn't easy because they're quite heavy. I hold mine for a while. It feels good in my hand, smooth and cool. There is a hole in it, right in the middle and I look through it. *Bierschenk, you're dead*. I don't know who said it, the teacher, I think. All the others had of course already thrown theirs and were pointing fingers at me. I am so used to it by now, to be singled out. It's all for the team, not for the individual. And as has been pointed out repeatedly by teachers, I'm not a good team player.

Bomb

There are some teachers who regularly tell us that War is coming, and every few weeks we do a nuclear drill. It's an urgent, wailing sound that breaks the boredom in the classroom and makes us all jump. We're allowed to take our bags and coats with us and have three minutes to get down to the basement. Sometimes I'm so scared of war I don't want to go to school, for fear that the Bomb will drop while I'm in class. I practice running home in under three minutes to see if I could make it, because if it happens, I want to be with my family. Then again, I also need to think of my little sister who's at the daycare on

the other side of the village. I need to get to her first. It's a tricky decision: with whom do I want to die? My parents and grandparents or my little sister? It would be unfair to leave her at the daycare when the Bomb drops. I decide that, when the time comes, I will run to the daycare in under three minutes, so at least she won't be alone. And I don't want to die in the school basement with all those people I don't really care about that much. I try not to think about War, but sometimes, the fear gets so bad that I keep asking my mother. *Mama, will there be war, will there really be war.* And she says, *Do you really think these politicians want to die? Because if they start that war, that special war, they will. Everyone would die.*

There will be no war, I promise you, there will be no war.

America

I am watching a programme about a North American national park on the West German channel. It's in black and white, but that doesn't stop me from being completely engrossed by the expanse, the vastness, the mountains, the rivers, all that space, and people speaking English. By the time the programme finishes I'm crying. I'm crying like someone just died and my mother rushes to comfort me and asks me what is wrong. *I will never see these places, I will never travel anywhere, not while I'm young. Oh, but you will*, says my mother and holds me, *I promise you, you will.* I cry on my mother's neck for a long time and hope they will never let her travel to the West, because I'm so afraid she won't come back.

Shaka Zulu

One of my favourite programmes on the West German Channel is Shaka Zulu. It's a true story and I cannot miss any of the episodes.

I have to make sure that I am at home every Saturday afternoon at five so I can watch it. Maybe I can travel to Africa one day, because our country is friends with Angola. I could be an ethnologist in Angola! The day of the very last episode, my father comes home carrying a new television. *Surprise!* he shouts, and my mother and I nearly fall over backwards. It's a colour television! How my father did it, how he hustled that one, he won't tell us. A colour television costs 6000 East German Marks, an almost phenomenal amount of money. But that is beside the point for me.

I can watch the last episode of Shaka Zulu in colour. Because my father takes a long time to set everything up, I am missing the beginning and am starting to panic, but then, something happens: the picture slowly emerges on the screen, filling it with a yellow hue, then green, then full colour. My parents, grandparents, sister and I are sitting in front of this magic apparatus like the first humans watching a solar eclipse. So this is what it looked like all along, so colourful? I cannot believe how even more beautiful King Shaka looks on a colour TV. His skin, his adornments, the landscape! In the end, to my horror, Shaka is killed and deep red blood fills his mouth and spills down the sides. I cry and cry and cry and my mother, as usual, tries to make it go away by telling me it's only an actor and that he's fine.

Rabies

The street from our house leads uphill into the deep, lush forest. I love walking up the hill. We call it "Hay Mountain". From the top of Hay Mountain, you can overlook the valley and the village cradled in its centre. I spot our house and wonder how come that that's where I live, why I was born, and why am I the way I am. When I walk up Hay Mountain, I always carry a wooden stick, and I'm aware of everything going on around me. Sometimes, I go a little bit further than the lookout, but as soon as I see the yellow warning sign with the image of a fox's head in the middle "Warning. Restricted area. Rabies!" That's when I turn around and head back. Rabies is everywhere in this forest. I know not to touch any wild animals. I know not to pick up baby rabbits or foxes, no matter how cute and tame they appear.

Deliverance

Look out the window, my mother calls as she comes running into the kitchen. I am still eating breakfast and she motions me to the window. A deer is stumbling down the street, past our house. It trembles, shrieks like a human, then collapses at the end of the street near the post box, its body twisting and shaking. I hold my breath, I cannot look away, and a big lump works its way up my throat and escapes in a gasp. The neighbours opposite watch from their gate until one of them takes off on his moped, probably to get the forest ranger. When the ranger finally arrives in his green Lada Niva, he gets out, slowly walks up to

the twitching deer, looks at it way too long and then whacks it over the head with the end of his rifle. My mother says that death came as a release to the deer, because rabies is incurable. But how is death a release?

Nothing bad will happen

Then one day, rabies comes into our house. My father's friend, the vet is sitting at the kitchen table. My father is standing with his back to the window, and my mother is leaning against the sink, arms folded, shaking her head and not smiling. They're not chatting and joking as usual. I drop my bag on the floor and my mother says, *Don't touch Papa; and Opa, don't touch Opa either!*

A few days ago, my father and grandfather slaughtered one of our sheep because it was sick, and to be on the safe side, my father called for the vet who took some samples from the sheep's brain. Now we know the sheep had rabies and all the other sheep need to be killed. My father and grandfather have to drive to another city every day to a special clinic to get rabies injections. They have to go there seventeen times in a row, first thing in the morning. I am scared for them both, but my father says the injections will help, nothing bad will happen. I don't dare hug him for a few days. My mother burns the rabid sheep's hide in a big fire in the garden, and then she remembers that she saw our cat chewing on it. So now, the cat must be killed, too. Our neighbour offers to do the job. My father puts the cat inside a canvas bag and they go to the field up the road. The neighbour always likes to make a bit of a show and tells my father to let the

cat out of the sack, which he does. Several shots echo over the field, the cat escapes in great leaps towards the forest and is never seen again. For weeks, I watch our dog and our rabbits closely. Do they froth at the mouth? Are they particularly thirsty? Do they tremble? I am not sure if I should touch them at all. Finally, my father has enough. He grabs our dog and hugs him tight, rubbing his face in the dog's face, who is delighted by all this attention. *So*, he says, *do you think I would do this if I thought the dog had rabies?*

Mayday

Every year, on the night before the first of May, my father and I get up at four in the morning. He prepares sandwiches, a flask of tea, packs some apples. My mother is up too, because she needs to make sure I am dressed warmly enough. We greet the month of May by walking towards it, toward the sunrise and into the forest. We need to be back before noon, because we also have to go to the Mayday demonstration in the village square. If we don't go, the local policeman or some Party busybody will report our absence. My father has instructed my mother to hang out the red flag before 7 o'clock in the morning, because otherwise there'll be a warning again, like last year. But all that is so unimportant to me. I'm awake, so awake, my stomach tickles, my hands cannot stay still. It's only when we start walking uphill, towards Hay Mountain, dark and mighty over the valley, that I calm down and keep up with my father's steady pace. He knows all the secret paths and hideouts in the woods. Will we see wild animals, birds,

find anything interesting along the way? I'm with my father and I'm not afraid of rabies this time. We walk up the narrow gravel path to Hay Mountain and my heart leaps at every noise in the undergrowth. I look at every move my father makes; when he raises his finger to his lips and points at something, when he stops and motions me to duck. There's a wild boar ploughing the loose forest soil for roots, a herd of wild goats tramples past. We find deer tracks and fox tracks in the mud. The birds are waking up and the morning sunlight trickles through the gaps between the trees. The sunlight also reveals rubbish dumps all over the forest. Discarded barrels, car batteries, washing machines, empty bottles. *Look at this*, says my father, and shakes his head, *look at this*. Suddenly, thick raindrops patter down on us. *A spring shower*, my father laughs, *it'll make you grow!*

He tells me to shelter under a tree while he quickly gathers branches and twigs. Within minutes, he has built us a little hut, padded with leaves and we sit inside, out of the rain, share an apple, and he gives me his boyish smile. I look at him and a wave of warmth runs through me. This is my father.

Earth

My mother throws a lump of clay onto the slowly rotating potter's wheel, flicks the black switch on the side that is crusted with dried clay, and the motor wails and howls, creaks and shudders, while the wheel goes faster and faster. My mother's hands cover the lump of clay, holding it down, pushing a hole in the middle. Then her fingers slowly pull up the sides of the

clay lump. She dibs tiny grooves into it and within minutes, there is the first of what will be five hundred beer kegs. She then separates the keg from the wheel with a metal thread and places it on one of the shelves to dry. Everything she does, each of her moves, is so certain, so secure, knowing. She paints flowers or patterns onto the kegs. Her fingers never shake. I like watching her hands work and remember how cool they feel on my forehead when I have a fever.

Music is playing on the small dusty radio on the windowsill. On cold days, the small iron furnace near the door heats up the workshop. I sit near the oven and shape fantastic creatures from clay. I make an ashtray for my father, or a woman's head.

My mother works late into the night from early in the morning. People from all over come to buy her ceramics, because it's something unusual in this country. Not many people have their own businesses, and pottery is very rare. I am proud that my mother can do this, that she is an artist. But as secure and steady as her hands are, the kegs and bowls and cups she makes and paints can be moody. When the furnace has been packed with them and burns through the night, at a thousand degrees, you never know what you will find when you open the furnace door. Sometimes, many of the beautiful clay things are broken or burst. The furnace is unpredictable. But most of the time, they turn out fine, and the furnaces's heat fills the workshop and the clay things go ting, ting, ting.

Housebook

Every once in a while, the doorbell rings late in the evening around my bedtime. Then my mother sighs and says, *It's Frau Hege*. Frau Hege has something to do with bureaucracy, or the Socialist Unity Party, or both. When she comes around, my parents get all fiddly and nervous and rummage around in the forbidden drawer, where they keep all the important paperwork like our passports and social security documents. Frau Hege checks all the paperwork and takes notes in neat handwriting. She also checks the Housebook. The Housebook has to be filled in correctly and meticulously, because this is where all visitors need to be recorded, particularly visitors from West Germany. And because we get a lot of visitors from West Germany, it takes Frau Hege a long time to check everything. My parents are always especially nice to Frau Hege, and I also make sure I greet her nicely, before I go to bed. I don't know why, but somehow, I always feel a little guilty when Frau Hege comes, as if I have done something wrong, and I don't know about it yet. Frau Hege has incredibly fascinating teeth: they are yellow with a brownish tint, and very big. One particularly long tooth on the top right is golden and framed by a silvery rim. When she speaks, there is a faint clicking sound coming from that tooth. She stays long into the night. Sometimes, when I start from my sleep because of a bad dream, I can still hear her voice and the clicking coming from the kitchen.

Preparation

Whenever I see blood, the palms of my hands get cold and sweaty. Panic builds up somewhere down in my stomach, works its way up to my throat, and spreads to my forehead. Then I know, not much longer, here it comes, the big darkness that pulls a black hood over my face and hangs me upside down a cliff. And because one thing I hear a lot from the adults around me is, *You are too sensitive, you are like a mimosa, you need to toughen up, you need to get a thicker skin*, I decide to do just that and join the Young Paramedics. It's one of the many after school activities we are obliged to join, on a voluntary basis, of course. The first thing we are equipped with is a uniform. We each get a first aid kit, and an instruction booklet, which I read front to back in one sitting. We learn to treat all injuries imaginable: cuts, burns, tears, open fractures, shattered bones, fractured skulls, knife wounds, bullet wounds. And I do not faint! I can do all the theory, I know exactly what to do. Then comes the day of the exam and if we pass, we can call ourselves certified Young Paramedics. For the exam, we need to take a compass and map and follow cues that lead us over the fields, over the river, into the woods. We arrive at a clearing and my heart nearly stops. The place is crowded with Extras who display remarkably realistic injuries of all kinds. There is a lot of fake blood, deep cuts, stomach wounds, and open fractures. Arms are torn open from wrist to elbow. I look for the most harmless wound and opt for a small kid with a long cut on his arm. Later on, the instructor reminds us, *Imagine this was an attack by the American aggressor. We need to be prepared.*

Baba

My great grandmother looks like she is two hundred years old. Small and skinny, her face like a white mask with two black holes for eyes and not a tooth left in her mouth. She always wears black and I am a little scared of her, because she does look a bit like Baba Yaga, the witch from the Russian fairy tales. I don't know if she knows who I am or what my name is, because she hardly says anything to me, and if she says something, it's in "Low German", the local dialect, which I can understand a little but not speak. She always sits in the same armchair in the kitchen, near the oven. Great grandmother lives with Aunt Marie and Uncle Alois. Marie has curly black hair and a kind face. Alois is always whistling; he talks very little, and I have never seen him without the stump of a cold cigar wedged in the corner of his mouth. I like the scent of the cigar and the smell of oil and metal in his workshop where he fiddles around with old car motors and repairs lawnmowers and washing machines. He's shown me photos of himself standing in front of a Russian tank with the top blown off. One day, my great grandmother doesn't sit in the armchair in the kitchen. She's lying in bed, in the backroom. The room is a dead room. There is nothing in it, just the bed, two chairs, a nightstand with a lamp, and a wooden cross on the wall. There are no flowers, no books, and no details that make a home. Great grandmother's head is barely visible in the big fluffy pillow. Grandmother sits there, cries silently, and prays. I sit there with her and look at this small, tired bundle of a woman in the bed. One day, the bed is empty. Grandmother and Aunt Marie go dressed in black for a year.

The calculator

Old people are allowed to travel to West Germany, so my grandparents go there as often as possible to visit relatives in Hessia. When they come back, they smell like a West German care parcel: a mix of freshly laundered clothes, warm bread, and coffee. I hug them tight and sniff their necks and clothes until grandmother says, *That's enough now*. My father says old people can travel to the West no problem, because it doesn't matter to our government if they come back or not; on the contrary. Of course, I need to keep this to myself. After one such visit to West Germany, my grandfather brings me a small pocket calculator in a leather sleeve. It is the best gift ever! And it runs on solar power, it never needs batteries! I need to know what it looks like on the inside. I just have to know. I'm going to open it and take a peek and then I'll put it back together. In a corner of my room, I carefully take out the tiny screws from the back of the calculator (I have a small screwdriver that I once borrowed from my father). I am not disappointed – the inside is a fantastic extra-terrestrial landscape of green and silver rivers, it looks like the map of another planet. The number keys drop to the floor and it's very fiddly to put them back where they belong. In the end, I cannot reassemble it. The screws have rolled under the cupboard. This is a catastrophe! This calculator is from "over there" and probably really expensive! I hide it under the carpet and after a while, I forget about it. Weeks later, my father is hoovering my room and discovers the dead calculator. He doesn't get mad at me. *You want to know things*, he says, *that's good*, and tussles my hair.

They're here

I'm pressing my cheek against the cool window pane so I can see as far down the street as possible. *Where are they? When are they coming? Shouldn't they be here already? What if they got into trouble at the border and they're not letting them through? What if the border guards found something illegal in the car and now they're already in prison and we'll never know?*

Then I hear the deep humming of what is clearly a Western car motor. *They're here!* I run out the front door, to the gate, just in time to see the light brown mighty Range Rover come up the street, dodging potholes. I know that every curtain behind every window in the neighbourhood is pulled aside this instant. My aunt, my uncle, my two cousins from West Berlin are here! My parents, my little sister and I are out on the street, waving at them as they park the car a bit further up, and then come running towards us. All the neighbours are looking. The welcoming ceremony goes on for minutes, hugs, kisses, tears, handshakes, laughter. They smell so good, so fresh, so new, tanned from their holidays in Italy or France. My cousin Anna casually throws back her hair that keeps falling over her eyes. She's wearing jeans with holes, intentional holes, and my cousin Marc sports an old army coat with a small West German flag on the side. They are older than me and by God, I want to look like them, I want to be them. They have an ease and coolness about them like only people from the West have. Their car is packed with clothes, shoes, fruit, juices, tinned goods, coffee and more coffee, sweets, chocolates, cocoa. All for us. For a whole week, we're living on a colourful island in an ocean of grey.

The American

My father's second cousin from Hannover will be visiting, and she's bringing her husband, who is from the USA! She's tried many times to come to visit and was always rejected, because of the American, but for my grandfather's eightieth birthday, the authorities have finally granted them permission to visit. Grandmother is sure no American has set foot in the village since 1945. I am beyond myself with pride and I tell everyone I know about the American, although my parents ask me to keep it quiet. I take out my sacred English textbook that is already stained and tattered, because I take it everywhere. I have no idea if I'm pronouncing the words right, but I learn long lists of vocabulary: refrigerator, hippopotamus, forceps, can, tomcat, and so on. How would I greet the American? My mother teaches me the phrase *I'm really glad to see you*. But how to say it: I'm *really* glad to see you. I'm really *glad* to see you! I'm really glad to see *you*.

The big day is a Saturday and I run home from school only to find three Western cars parked outside our gate. My mother is busy in the kitchen and smiles when she sees my flushed face. *They're upstairs*, she says and I run up to the first floor where my grandparents live. Everyone is assembled in the "good living room", my grandparents, some other relatives from the restricted zone and nearby West Germany, but I hardly see them. I only have eyes for the slim, short man who looks a bit lost in grandfather's favourite armchair. I go up to him, extend my hand and say, *I'm really glad to see you*.

Swartz

Bob the American has silvery hair and small, dark eyes behind very large round glasses. He is tanned, and his teeth are large and yellowish. Over the next couple of days, I follow Bob everywhere. I swallow up everything he says and he patiently corrects my English pronunciation. I am jealous of how his wife converses in English with such ease and I know this will probably be the only occasion in my whole life that I can hear English like this. I wish she'd leave us alone, so I can learn as much as possible, and luckily, she's busy most of the time with the two babies they've brought along. She didn't give birth to them: one is adopted from Honduras and the other one from El Salvador. Bob is so different in many ways. He's a nutritionist and only eats raw vegetables and grains, no bread, no milk, no honey, nothing that comes from animals. My grandparents cannot believe that he shuns their sausages and full-fat cakes, and it's beyond me how he manages to live on such little, limited food. Because there isn't much else to do in terms of amusement around here, we usually take our visitors for long walks through the forest, and Bob proves a very grateful excursionist. We walk across a meadow towards the woods and Bob stops every few minutes to point at grass and plants with a lot of ooh-ing and aah-ing. He picks leaves and eats them there and then, and all I can think of is how a rabid fox or badger might have salivated on just that leaf Bob is happily munching now.

On the last morning of his visit, I follow Bob into my grandparents' bathroom. He takes a small tin and carefully

unscrews the top, then shows it to me. *Look – Swartz*, he says. There's black powder in it that looks like ashes. He dips his toothbrush into the powder and then brushes his teeth, his large yellow teeth. With the powder they're now turning greyish yellow. He doesn't rinse his mouth.

He's a walking miracle to me and seems the opposite of a warmonger.

TRAVELS

You cannot choose your friends

My other grandmother, whom I call "Oma Oranienburg", lives in the largest Soviet military zone outside of the Soviet Union. Next to her house is the canal, and on the other side of the canal is the Soviet military airport. Her garden is one big adventure playground with apple trees, berry bushes, hideouts, a swing and a sandbox. I play in the garden all day, pick berries, watch birds, and build dens. I go fishing, frog hunting and build sandcastles on the small beach. When the Russian soldiers cycle along the other side of the canal, the forbidden side, I hide in the reeds and hold my breath as I watch them. Deep down, I wish they would spot me and call something to me in Russian. Officially, they are our brothers. My father says it's because you cannot choose your family and laughs and my mother gets angry when he says that. I love their melodious language and am proud when I can understand the odd word. It sounds nothing like the Russian we learn at school. When it gets dark, the military helicopters' deep humming fills the night and I sit behind the curtain with grandmother. We count the red and green flashing lights in the sky. It's scary, but scary in a good way. I feel safe knowing they're up there. With so many soldiers all around us, one has to feel safe. Grandmother doesn't think so, she says they're practicing for the third world war and I wish she wouldn't say that.

Murder mansion

When I'm staying at Oma Oranienburg's, she cycles to murder mansion every morning to get fresh breakfast rolls. It's still dark when she leaves the house, because she wants to beat the queue of people who all want rolls for breakfast, and the rolls are rationed. She cycles along the sandy path on the non-Russian side of the canal, and then turns left through a little foresty bit that is said to be haunted. Murder mansion is a tall, grey, three-story house. The facade is eaten away by the constant outpour of soot. One day, Oma says, *Let's cycle to murder mansion together*. The shop is one room on the ground floor which reeks of vinegar and mouldy potatoes. The shopping baskets are made of red plastic with sticky black handles and I don't want to touch them. All of the shelves are empty save one that is loaded with bags of flour. One of the bags is split open and there's flour all over the floor, but no one seems bothered. I don't know what we came in here for. I hope it's flour. Oma tells me a family used to live on the top floor and they were murdered, which of course happened a long time ago, probably before East Germany existed, because murder is something exclusively reserved for capitalist countries. The breakfast rolls from murder mansion are the best rolls in the world. They are small, oval shaped, crispy on the outside, fluffy, and warm on the inside. I bite a hole in it and dig out the dough with my fingers. I save a tiny bit for later, as fishing bait. Then I roll the dough into little shapes and eat them one by one. The rest of the bun I fill with butter and honey. Yes, the breakfast rolls from murder mansion are the best!

Oma Oranienburg

Her laughter is like seismic ripples. And it's contagious. We laugh until I have stitches and cannot breathe. I ask her, *Tell me about your life, tell me about when you were little, about the war, and tell me about the great flight.* And she tells me about the trail of people leaving her village in Pomerania, how she carried her baby, one of my aunts. She tells me about the bodies in the ditches. About her horse Hans who pulled the cart until he couldn't pull anymore. And how us, the Germans, deserved all this, for the horrible things we did. She never talks about East Germans and West Germans, only Germans, and I'm confused, because the East Germans are the *good* Germans, and the West Germans are the *bad* Germans, except our relatives who live there. They are the ones who didn't get rid of their Nazis like we did. She tells me everything about the war, also the things that were done to the women including herself, and which I do not really understand. She says the word *rape*, like she thinks I know what it means. But I don't. She says, *Neighbour's Ilse, she was only thirteen. Fifteen soldiers, fifteen.* I am not sure what exactly happened to Ilse but something stops me from asking for details. Oma puts her hands over her face and says, *Wat der Mensch aushält.* Sitting on the edge of the sofa, her hands now cupped before her, as if she's protecting an invisible small animal. She's twiddling her thumbs, and swaying while she talks. The swaying calms her down. I take her dry leathery hands in mine. *At night, I'm always scared*, she says. Oma is scared that she will do something wrong by accident, and that she'll be punished for it by the authorities. She's scared of filling in a form the wrong

way, or of saying something wrong to the wrong person. She's scared of soldiers, the police, the Stasi, lightning, and the cold. Once she jokingly called our head of state, Honecker, "Honni". I asked her, *Oh, can you call Erich Honecker that? That sounds funny!* She nearly cried begging me not to tell anyone, to please keep it to myself and she was only joking, it doesn't mean anything, anything at all.

A golden BMW

For the last few nights, Oma Oranienburg's insomnia got worse. It's understandable, because Opa Oranienburg has just died, even though his death seems like a relief not only to him but to her as well. She cannot sleep from the excitement that her only son is coming to visit from West Berlin. Her only son, who had been imprisoned by the Stasi and was then expatriated to West Berlin in exchange for a large amount of money, but I am not supposed to talk about this. Apparently it is some kind of business between West Germany and East Germany. Since East Germany sold my uncle to the West, he hasn't been allowed back in. I only know him from a photo: a young, thin man with very long hair and a leather jacket. He's holding his head up as if to say "What do you want?"

Oma tells me how she and my mother took the train shortly after my uncle got arrested. They had the address of this famous lawyer, scribbled on a piece of paper. This lawyer was a go-between, an inside-outsider who helped to get people into the West. *He had a golden BMW*, says Oma, *and a big house, full*

with things from the West. How is that possible, I want to know, how can he have all that stuff from the West if he lives here? I don't understand how all this works, how some things are possible in this country, where it's only about praise and punishment, miracles and catastrophes, but nothing in between.

For the wife

When the Russian soldiers cycle along the other side of the canal on their rusty bikes they're almost always laughing and joking. *It's their best time of the day*, says Oma, *when they can cycle along the canal.* When I go to town on Oma's ancient rusty bike, I pass the Russians barracks. I can see they have newspapers stuck to their windowpanes instead of curtains. One summer morning, I'm helping Oma in the garden. Everything is in full bloom, especially the roses. They're deep dark red, orange, yellow, white. Their scent makes you dizzy and the bees and butterflies seem drunk from their richness. Suddenly, a young Russian soldier is at the garden fence. *Privjet*, he says. He looks so young. His face is round and friendly. He points at a red rose. *Mozhno? Dlya zhenu?* It's the first time I hear this beautiful, strange language that I have become so used to and that is yet so alien to me outside of an official setting. It's the first time I meet a representative of our Big Brother in an unstaged situation, in real life, in an entirely human situation. My heart beats so loud in my chest, I want him to stay, to come in, and I want to hear more of this language.

For his wife, Oma, he wants a rose for his wife.

I know, says Oma, who all her life has been scared of men in general, and soldiers in particular. She cuts two or three roses and hands them to him over the fence.

Hungary is almost like being in West Germany

Once a year, we travel to Hungary. To me, Hungary is a little bit like being in West Germany, or what I imagine it to be, because there are so many West German tourists. We are not really supposed to talk to them, but my parents do it anyway. They make friends easily but are still careful, because, according to my father, the place is swarming with Stasi. I am not even sure who or what exactly the Stasi is, only that the grownups around me usually lower their voices when they say that word. I only know it's some kind of government agency. To me, it sounds kind of cute, the word, like any word ending in –i. But these are grown-up worries. The drive to Hungary is very, very long, because we have to drive through almost all of East Germany and the Czech Republic. At every border crossing there are hundreds of cars waiting, soldiers with machine guns, dogs, and my mother is always afraid they will arrest us, I don't know why. But as soon as we have crossed the Hungarian border, where the guards tip their hats and smile at us, the sky suddenly turns blue, my mother relaxes, and the country stretches before us, flat and wide and warm.

Spiders and Mosquitoes

We are staying in a one-room bungalow. The walls are white, soft, uneven, full of little dents. I like to run my fingers over them, and they feel like the cool soft skin of a gentle animal. We were lucky to get this bungalow, which only worked out because my mother knows someone who knows someone who owes someone a favour. There is just one problem. In every corner, every crevice of the room, there are big-bodied, black spiders. Every evening, my father has to get rid of every single spider, because otherwise, my mother cannot sleep. But the next morning, they are back, because after all, the bungalow is theirs. My father likes them, because they catch the mosquitoes that torment us as soon as the sun sets. In the evenings, we sit outside around the campfire with other tourists, and the men are swinging metal tins on strings around their heads. There is smoke coming from the tins, and it's supposed to scare away the mosquitoes. Nothing can get rid of them. The Balaton belongs to the spiders and mosquitoes. We are only visiting.

Bright yellow underpants

My father knows a secret bathing spot at the shores of Lake Balaton that's not occupied by East German nudists. Hidden behind bushes and reeds, there is a patch of sand near the shallow water, where I can play. Typical adults, my parents lie flat on their towels, facing the sun and proceed to talk about uninteresting things. Just as I'm getting ready to explore

the shore for frogs and snakes, I hear chatter and laughter in Hungarian, this beautiful language with words like endless strings of pearls. Three young girls with flowing, black hair, scramble through the reeds.

They walk into the lake with straight backs, fully clothed, their long colourful skirts swinging from side to side.

One of them carries an old tin bucket and drops it in the sand, before joining the others. Their wide blouses have flower prints and are soon completely drenched. I sit in the sand and stare at them, as they laugh and splash each other with water, washing their thick black hair in the lake. They have a way about them, so sure, so matter-of-fact-like. The sky, the sun, the water, it belongs to them and they are part of it. For a split second, I wonder if these three girls are real or if they are spirits of the lake, water people, and we have found their haunting place. The girls wave in my direction as if they're asking me to join them but I dare not move. I just want to sit in the sand and look at how beautiful they are. The reeds are rustling and a group of small half naked children, maybe four or five of them, not much older than me, are running past us, cheering and shrieking; water splashes onto the little beach and droplets of lake rain onto me. The children are all wearing bright yellow underpants. I am in awe of how the older girls go bathing in their clothes. And when they finally come out, slowly, their skirts are heavy with water, they just leave their clothes on, and their hair glistens in the sun, black waterfalls down their backs. They walk away, parting the reeds for the horde of small children that follows them. I look over at my mother who has her eyes closed. My father is reading. They seem oblivious to the whole scene.

Was I the only one who saw them? Maybe they were ghosts after all? Three mermaids and their flock. One thing I know, if I was bathing in my clothes, my mother would get really mad, make me get changed instantly and rub me dry for fear I'd catch a cold, even in thirty degrees Celsius, like today. I want to be as beautiful as those girls are, when I am older. I want to walk as they do, with a colourful skirt swinging around my legs, a black, glistening waterfall down my straight back. I know this will probably never happen, because I have hair like my father, blond, light and thin, like feathers. I look at the wet footprints in the sand they've left behind and then I see something bright yellow in a muddy puddle nearby. A flash of excitement – an abandoned pair of bright yellow underpants! At least I could have those, and be a little bit like these mermaid children! Just as I am about to put them on, my mother's voice cuts through the hot summer air: *Absolutely not!*

The uncle

My parents managed to get a spot in a youth hostel in the Czech Republic, in the Tatra Mountains. Whenever we go abroad, that is, to Poland, Hungary or the Czech Republic, we usually bring our tent on the rooftop of the car, because it's impossible to find a place to stay that has an actual roof. You have to apply years in advance or know someone who owes you a favour. Not many people seem to owe my parents favours. But this time we were lucky, and we leave in our Trabant in the middle of the night, so we can make it to the Czech order by early morning. As usual,

my mother has tucked me in on the back seat. I am buried underneath a duvet, because she is always worried that I may get cold and become ill. I try to stay awake but the motor's humming puts me to sleep. I'm awakened by a light, a very strong light that someone is shining in my face. A young looking man with a round, friendly face and a soldier's cap is looking at me. *Just one child?* he says, with a strong accent.

I sit up and look out the back window. We are in a long long line of cars, so this must be the border. There must be hundreds of cars behind us. The noise from the Trabant, Warturg and Lada engines fill the night air. We arrive at our destination at dusk, and I can see the Tatra mountains, all grey and rugged, dotted with trees. Our room in the youth hostel is small, with a bunk bed and a single bed, one table, two chairs and a piano stool that I sit on and twirl around. My mother seems nervous as she unpacks and my father smokes a cigarette at the open window. There is a knock on the door and my mother rushes to open it. A man is standing outside and I know right away who it is, because I have seen his face in many photos. My mother shrieks and throws her arms around him. He has my grandmother's Slavic eyes.

That's your uncle Michael, from West Berlin, says my father and flicks his cigarette out the window.

WEST

Drills

The specially chartered school bus stops outside the gate bearing a sign that reads "Machine Tractor Station".

The Machine Tractor Station hosts machinery for collective farms. It's a grey, dirty, run down place. Two red-nosed workers are standing near the gate, smoking. They are our official role models and heroes, in rubber boots and blue work clothes. The courtyard is covered in potholes filled with oily rainwater. The teacher calls us to order and leads the way to the grey seminar building. We leave our coats and bags in one of the stuffy, cold classrooms and proceed to pick out damp-smelling work clothes and hairnets from a pile that someone has left on the teacher's desk. Then, our instructor comes to collect us. He's a short, dark haired, moustachioed man in a camouflage uniform. He tells us that, after class, he's heading off to field training with the "Combat Group of the Working Class", our country's paramilitary reserve force. He leads us to the work hall lined with noisy machines and mounted electric drills in all shapes and sizes. He tells us that we can be proud because, as of today, we will gain first-hand experience of what it means to contribute to the socialist production. I am put to work on one of the small electric drills and my task for the day is to deburr drilled holes in small pieces of metal. The student next to me drills holes into a metal square, throws them into a box placed between us, I pick out the metal square and deburr the drill hole. For the first ten minutes, I'm enjoying this, because it's so simple and I can't do anything wrong, plus, I don't have to talk to anyone. I take piece by piece, put it on the block under

the drill, and then lower the drill into the small hole to get rid of the sharp metal bits that are sticking out on the sides. I have no idea what these parts are and what they are used for. Each of us is drilling or deburring some kind of metal part. After a while it gets so monotonous and boring, and the noise in the work hall settles inside my head and will make my ears ring for hours after. I feel numb, numb towards everything. The teacher observes us, does his round, asks each of us if we're okay, which is usually a rare thing to hear from our teachers. I ask him what these metal blocks are for. He winks at me and says, *Parts for the SS20, but that's confidential*. SS20s are, of course, nuclear warheads. We drill, we deburr, and we go on our break. After I don't know how many hours, we go to the classroom for our lesson called "Introduction to socialist production". I don't understand any of it, but I know for the final exam, I'll just learn the whole book by heart and that's that.

Forbidden

I'm going through the stuff in the forbidden drawer in the living room cupboard. It's where my parents keep important documents and what little jewellery my mother has. There is also stationary with flowers, and a small pouch with West German money in it, that I count and recount. I know some of this belongs to me, but my parents keep it safe. The drawer smells good, of paper and leather. There is my social security pass. A small red booklet with the hammer and sickle in a wreath of wheat, the East German symbol. My little sister has doodled

all over it. This booklet is as old as I am, here is the date of my birth and the first stamp of my life, to confirm, I was born. That was thirteen years ago. A lot is happening at the moment. More and more people are leaving for the West and my mother wants to go, more than ever. I want to go to secondary school next year, so I can get my Abitur and study at University. But the headmaster has already told me that, should I decide to continue going to church and not participate in the youth initiation ceremony of the GDR, then I would not be able to go to secondary school. The ceremony is voluntary, but it is bound to certain consequences. And the consequence for me is to end up on a chicken farm, or drilling holes into metal bits in a factory for the rest of my life. So, I will probably end up doing what everyone does. Pretend I believe in the right thing, in the "cause". I decide to write a letter to Oma Oranienburg and pull out the stationery. A sheet of paper falls to the floor. I recognise my father's handwriting. I read: "After long consideration my family and I have decided to apply for expatriation to West Berlin". I feel all my internal organs gathering in a collective jolt. My parents have done it, they have really done it. This is a draft for an application to leave East Germany.

Stay here

You can start packing up your books, says my mother. Supposedly, we're leaving for the West in four weeks. We need to take care of everything now, need to sell everything, pack everything up. So it's really happening. I remember that time when my parents

and I stood in front of the Fence and I couldn't believe I would never touch the grass on the other side. I was a different person then. Now things have changed and I don't want to go, I don't want to go to the West, because what if our teachers and our government is right? What if they are right and the West is full of warmongering, deceiving capitalists, murder and drug addiction? Aren't we happy enough in our little bubble East Germany? But most importantly, I am in love for the first time and I am pretty sure that I will never again be as happy as I am now, or as unhappy.

But what if you and he fall out next week? says my mother. She suggests we can write letters and maybe even visit each other when we're older. But I know that once we leave this country, they will never, ever allow us back in. *Stay here*, he says, *you can live with your grandparents*. I know this won't work. I know my mother is right, and we will eventually fall out with each other. I know I will end up going to the West, no matter how scared I am.

In the socialist sense

My mother was right. And like every time, when it turns out she is right, she says the inevitable words "I told you so". Not long after I told my first love that we would be leaving for West Germany soon, things started dying down. It was only natural, because the looming exit from this country put a "best before" date on our childish relationship before it really got anywhere. And there is more. Shortly after I discovered the fateful letter

in the forbidden drawer, my father got expelled from school. *I am no longer tolerable in the socialist sense*, he told us, imitating the headmaster who said these exact words to him in a kind of show trial at school. Most of my father's colleagues vouched for him and asked the headmaster to keep my father on until our departure, but no chance. He now works illegally, as a car mechanic in a friend's shop. *Because if there is one good thing in this country*, he says, *it's that everyone has to learn a trade, even if they become a doctor or lawyer or whatever after.* I am moving between prides: that we are now a little bit like enemies of the state; but also fear of a new life in the West. Autumn is here and that doesn't help. Things are slowing down, the days are getting shorter. Puberty is hard enough, falling in and out of love is hard enough. Grasping the definiteness of this new thing that I cannot even name is hard enough. I just know there is one last thing I want to do, and that is to join the Free German Youth – the youth organization for pupil's age fourteen onwards. And the reason I want to do that is because the inauguration ceremony takes place in the former concentration camp Buchenwald, near Weimar, now a memorial site. It will be the last time I get to travel in a bus through Thuringia, together with my classmates. It's the last time I can take in the place I come from. For the ceremony, we need to each buy a blue shirt with the rising sun emblem on the sleeve and the letters FDJ. My parents refuse to buy one, so I borrow it from a neighbour. It doesn't have the emblem on it, and my father says I can just fold my arms before me, and no one will notice.

Buchenwald

When I show up outside the school where my classmates are gathered waiting for the bus to Buchenwald, all conversation stops. The head teacher shakes her head but doesn't send me home. Why I'm doing this, no one understands. During the trip, I sit alone on a window seat and drink in the landscape. It's a long drive to Weimar, because the roads are so bad and the bus cannot go very fast. We have to stop every once in a while, because a few of the others get car sick and have to step out to throw up. I have enough time to dream and reminisce and all of a sudden, out of nowhere comes a little sting of joy and excitement. Maybe, the West isn't so bad. Maybe, if things go well, I'll be able to travel to other countries. Maybe it'll all be one big adventure, and who knows, one day, I might be able to come back, and I'll be wearing clothes from the West, I'll throw back my hair like my cousin from West Berlin.

The little sting of joy settles somewhere in my chest and I beg it to stay there, at least for a bit.

At the Buchenwald memorial site we are ushered into a small room that is so hot and stuffy, I can hardly breathe. We are gathered around a model of the camp, and our guide, a small, pale woman with very blond hair proceeds to tell us about the history of Buchenwald, about the atrocities committed here, and only a few minutes into her talk, everything goes dark around me.

I come to on a bunk bed in a bleak, cold room with bare walls. There is no one around. So I fainted again, and my head hurts so much, my legs and arms feel like they weigh a ton.

The door opens and my teacher comes in with a glass of water and another blanket. She shakes her head. *In all my years as a teacher, you are the first pupil who has come here by choice.* She tells me to rest and only comes to get me when it is time to take the oath. So now I am a member of the Free German Youth. Only one week later, in a bout of collective rebellion, I and a few others leave our membership cards on the floor outside the headmaster's office. A few very brave older students burn their blue shirts outside the school building, late in the evening. It is the first week in November, 1989, the country is in turmoil, people are out on the streets every Monday night in Leipzig, East Berlin, Erfurt, demonstrating for change, people get beat up by police and arrested, hundreds of East Germans have fled on foot into Austria over the Hungarian border, thousands of East Germans have squatted the West German embassy in Prague. All this happened while we carried on in this village at the edge of the world. And according to my mother, we might be leaving for the West in about a week.

The fence is just a fence

It's around three in the morning as we finally reach the official border crossing point between Thuringia in the GDR and Hessia, West Germany. We have spent the last six hours driving in a convoy of rattling and stinking two-stroke engine cars through a country that has not been the same since yesterday. We're scared and nervous, because we're not really sure what's going to happen. But then we see the East German border

guards and we can see their uniforms are adorned with flowers. They even have flowers stuck in the barrels of their machine guns. They're smiling and just waving us through; we don't even need to show our passports. They've given up on that, there's too many of us. The stinking, noisy, endless traffic jam is squeezing through to the other side, and nothing, nothing can stop it. We're driving through the open checkpoint, just like that, and the fence is just a fence now. *Children, we're on the other side, we are in the West!* And on the other side, in the West, there are people lining the street, they're clapping and laughing and shouting welcome, they're banging on our car roof, grabbing my mother's hand through the open car window, patting my father on the shoulder. They're passing us bags with sandwiches, water, sweets, and toys. My parents are crying and laughing. My mother turns around to us and squeezes my hand. In the lights of the cars behind us I can see how wet her face is. I'm holding my little sister on my lap, who's clapping and shrieking with joy. I hold her very tight, as if she could turn into a little bird and just fly out of the window into this unknown, new world. I hold on to her, because I'm afraid I might wake up any moment and everything will be as it has always been. *Claudia, weinst du?* she says, unbelievingly, and I say, *I am happy, I am crying because I am happy.* If this is possible, if this really is possible then maybe I can even go to America. I look at the people on the side of the road, looking at us. I see and feel no suspicion, no hatred, no fear, no condescension, no insecurity. There is only joy.

EPILOGUE

Just looking

My father wants to go on a little outing to the patrol path, where the fence used to be. Just looking. That's the new favourite pastime of all East Germans. Just going "over there" to what used to be the West and have a look. Pop into McDonald's and dream of the USA, which has suddenly become a possibility, even though hardly anyone has the money for a ticket. A lot of people go to where the fence used to be. Some of it is still there. Souvenir hunters have been cutting bits out of it and selling it on flea markets. We pass the former checkpoint. The little house is empty, the red and white barrier no longer there. I wonder what happened to the two grey-green soldiers. Are they unemployed now? Are they going to find another job? Who would want to hire someone who did service at the border, the worst ever job. My father steers our Lada up the steep hill towards the patrol way that consists of large concrete slabs and runs like a sore across the field towards the forest. He stops the car. We get out and stand there, overlooking the valley, the thick forest, the concrete slabs. My mother is getting worried and wonders if this is legal. East Germany still exists, after all, what if there are mines here? What if we get arrested, shot at? My father just scoffs. *If there were mines here, there'd be a sign*. We take a few steps into the forest, where I spot a green metal box on a pole. It has a telephone painted on it. My father walks straight over to it, lifts the flap and a male voice says, *Ja?* The voice sounds a little hesitant, uncertain. My father seems surprised. He holds the flap and stares into the box, as if looking for a little man in there. I hold my breath, because I

am sure my father will say something nasty, like "kiss my arse", or worse. This would be his chance to put all those years of restrictions, frustration, doubts, fears, into one sentence to one of the orderlies of the state he hated so much.

My father moves his face closer to the box and says, *Never mind, comrade.*

Thank you to my parents for giving me the best of all worlds, filled with stories. To my sister, for all the laughs. To Michael Curran of Tangerine Press for making this happen, and for simply being great to work with. To Pete Lally for being the first to publish my work and for his valuable feedback on the early version of this manuscript. To Hosho McCreesh for his encouragement and friendship. Thank you to Andrej, from the Far East, for reminding me that life always has a surprise ready. Last but not least, my thanks go to Dr. Slava Fomenko, in far away Magadan, Russia for his valuable thoughts on my writing.

Claudia Bierschenk was born near East Berlin and grew up in Thuringia, in the former East Germany. She studied English, Spanish, and Political Sciences in Germany and Ireland. She learnt Russian in Moscow, worked as a volunteer in Israel and was a teaching assistant in Chile. From 2004 to 2008, she lived and worked in Derbyshire and South Yorkshire in the UK, where she started writing fiction and poetry. Her work has been published in a number of independent literary magazines. Ms Bierschenk lives in Berlin.

Pete Lally lives on the island of Gozo with his partner, daughter and two dogs. In 2012 he formed Pig Ear Press, through which he produces limited run books made using traditional printing and binding techniques. Books from the press can be found in museums and galleries around the world as well as in private collections.

July 2022

This first edition is published as a trade paperback; there are 126 numbered & lettered copies signed by the author, & handbound in boards by the Tangerine Press, Tooting, London; lettered copies also contain signed artwork by Hans Ticha.